Inward Holiness

Carla Burton

©2018 Carla Burton

Gallatin, TN

Cover Design by Mandy DeHart Designs

All Scripture quotations in this book are from the King James Version of the Bible with emphasis added by the author.

All rights reserved. No portion of this publication may be reproduced, stored in an electronic system, or transmitted in any form or by any means, electronic, mechanical, photocopy, recording, or otherwise, without prior permission of Carla Burton.

ISBN-13: 978-1983981265

DEDICATION

To my husband, Kurtis, who preaches and lives inward holiness everyday!

Contents

1	Inward Holiness—What exactly *is* that?.....................	11
2	Inward Holiness is Essential for Salvation................................	21
3	Standards for Inward Holiness..................................	27
4	Fruits of Inward Holiness..................................	53
5	The Next Step........................	61

Inward holiness will produce *outward fruits*

but *outward holiness* will be

the evidence of *inward change*!

Chapter 1

Inward Holiness—What exactly *is* that?

Remember The Order

As we continue in this process called *holiness* we want to remember the importance of following the order that God set forth. He is not a God of chaos but He shows us over and over again that order is important to Him. If order is important to God in all the others areas such as salvation, creation, rainfall and the solar system, then why would we think that God would not have an order to holiness. He does and it's our responsibility to follow that order with the same diligence that we give to the order of the plan of salvation. The order of holiness is Attitude, Principle & Standard, which we discussed in our last booklet, "Steps to Holiness".

But just as God has an order to how we overall receive and follow holiness, He also has an order for us to produce the fruits of holiness in our lives. The cleanup of our lives always begins inwardly before the fruit is produced outwardly. That is why the second booklet in this series will focus on teaching us about inward holiness principles and standards. And as we follow these, we *will* see a change outwardly. So let's begin to walk this path.

Soul *and Spirit*

Inward holiness is allowing your "inward parts" to obey the Word of God and produce a change in your heart and mind. It is allowing the Spirit of God to begin this renovation of our lives from inside of us. It involves both the ***spirit*** and ***soul*** of someone being transformed. I believe that there is a misconception regarding these 2 parts of us. We have a tendency to believe that perhaps they are the same thing, and often we use the word to describe both the spiritual and the natural part of man. In I Thessalonians 5:23 Paul tells us that they are 2 distinctly separate parts of us. So let's define each of them, so that we can have a better understanding and work to cleanse ourselves properly from the inside out.

The **soul** is a person's mind, will, and emotions. Is is the natural part of the spirit man. The soul is driven by the five senses: touch, sight, smell, hearing, and seeing. It is the part of us that reacts or responds in our natural body to something we absorb through our 5 senses.

The **spirit** is the part of a person that was given to us by the breath of God and is that portion of Him in our lives always seeking a reconnection to His divine presence. It is the spiritual part of man that is directly connected to God. The spirit was the part of us that died immediately in the Garden of Eden but can be reborn immediately by the quickening (resurrection) of our spirits with the infilling of His Spirit.

From the beginning, we were designed that our soul and spirit would guide our actions. In the garden of Eden, Adam and Eve's actions were driven by their soul and spirit. Before they ate of the tree, each day their spirit was touched by the Spirit of God. Each day the Spirit of God would come down into the garden of Eden and His Spirit would communicate and touch the spirit of Adam and Eve. Genesis 3:8 tells us that God came down and walked in the cool of the day. This had to be a familiar time and event for Adam and Eve, because this was the one time that something was different. Whereas before, they would run to be in the presence of God, this time they hid themselves. This communion between the holy Spirit of God and the natural spirit of man seemed to be a daily occurrence. And this time that God and man spent together allowing their spirits to confer helped Adam to make right decisions and follow a righteous path. So their spirit would receive guidance from His Spirit and then in turn, their spirit's would control their soul, or their mind, will and emotion. The soul then in turn controlled the body and any actions that it would take.

The sadness of Genesis 3 is that the serpent didn't tell Eve the complete truth. When he and Eve began their conversation, he called her attention to how good and pleasant the fruit of that one forbidden tree looked and asked her why they weren't eating of this tree. She tells him that God said that they would die. Now we truly see how deceitful Satan is because he only tells us a half truth. Genesis 3:4, *"And the serpent said unto the woman, Ye shall not surely die:"* He was halfway correct in that they didn't immediately fall down dead, but he left out the part about something that did immediately die – their spirit man. You see when sin enters into the heart of man, there is an immediate disconnect (death) between you and the Spirit of God. This is why after they had eaten of the tree of knowledge of good and evil, their spirit's actually died to the control of His Spirit. The whole story of the Bible is about God's search for a way to heal that breach so that His Spirit could once again lead and guide our actions.

Many people ask the question about how and why the world could become as evil as it is today. They ask how we could devolve to a state where we do such cruel, hateful and even murderous things to each other. But the root can be traced back to the place where we disconnected our spirit man from God. Without His Spirit leading and guiding us, our flesh will rule us to the point that we will do things we would never have considered before. We see this immediately played out in Genesis 4 because when Cain did not work to keep his spirit connected to God, his jealousy caused him to kill his own brother. We need to realize that without God's Spirit active in our lives daily, that we **will sin**.

The design was that our spirit man would communicate daily with God's Spirit. And through this interaction, we would receive wisdom, understanding and direction to be able to make proper decisions that would please Him. This *spirit* connection would produce a proper *soul* (mind, will, emotion) action in our physical body.

So how does our soul (mind, will, emotions) control our physical bodies? A good example is if your hand touches a hot burner on the stove. Your soul (your mind), tells your emotions that something is wrong. Then the pain (emotions) kick in because you actually feel the burn. Then you pull your hand quickly (your will) from the burner. All of this can happen in mere seconds but the process always remains the same. Our soul, this mind, will and emotional part of us, has always controlled whatever actions we produced in our lives. But let's look at this in regards to a spiritual actions. A man sees a woman that he is attracted to. No sinful behavior at this point, because God designed and created us with these feelings and emotions. But if this man's spirit has not been connecting to God's Spirit, then his whole way of controlling what happens from this point on is only according to his fleshly desires or will. The key to the outward actions of this man being right in the eyes of God, is totally dependent upon how much of God's Spirit he has allowed to connect to his own spirit.

This is why man has never been able to govern himself *even with* laws and punishment. Our spirits are tainted and because of this it taints everything else in the downward line, our souls and our actions. You can see this in the progression of dispensations. When man tried to govern himself, following the cleansing of the earth after Noah, it wasn't too long before they were right back where they had started. We cannot govern ourselves without our spirit being touched by His Spirit and then allowing that Spirit to control our soul – our mind, will and emotions. We need the Spirit of God active in our lives and directing and guiding our every actions. This is the importance of beginning our holiness process by cleansing the inward parts of us first.

God's Desire

In Psalm 51:6, David acknowledges God's desire for our lives. He says to the Lord, *"Behold, thou desirest truth in the **inward** parts...."* Once again, we see that yearning desire of God to reconnect with His people **Spirit** to **spirit.** We were created from the beginning with our main purpose being this daily connection and fellowship with God. And when our relationship was killed by sin, a holy God knew He could not come near us until we changed who we were. This holiness process is all about receiving His Spirit, conforming to His Spirit daily and then becoming more like Him. In I Peter 1:16 God lays out this desire for us by saying, *"Be ye holy; for I am holy."* I hear not a commandment in that statement, but I hear a *yearning*, from a Holy God for a chance to reconnect to His creation. I hear the very reason that He suffered on Calvary in this statement. God did everything *He* could to design a plan where we could actually do I Peter 1:16. This holy God could ***not*** co-exist with sin or unrighteousness. And the death that occurred in the Garden of Eden was this daily, consistent communication. But the beauty is that God designed a plan, that if we follow, He can then have communion with us once again. And with His Spirit guiding us we can become holy and live in holiness, being a "living sacrifice" that is "acceptable" to the Lord (Romans 12:1).

So we need to understand the difference between our spirit and our soul. And then we need to make sure that we are connecting both back in the right manner so that our lives can be guided by His Spirit. And through this connection, our actions will follow what is pleasing to Him!

Inward Holiness before Outward Holiness

To be sure that we are producing the fruit of holiness in the proper manner, we are going to make sure that we clean up the inside first. So let's go back to the Bible and make sure that we have this order correct.

Jesus told the Pharisees that they must clean up their spirits for their outward holiness to count towards righteousness. Jesus says in Matthew 23:26, *"Thou blind Pharisee,* ***cleanse first that which is within*** *the cup and platter, that the outside of them may be clean also."* Jesus tells them that where they begin in this process in ***within*** or inside. The Pharisees were a devoutly religious sect of that day. But they were consumed with the outward signs of being religious. The ceremonies of washing their hands, how they gave their offerings, the pomp and circumstances of who ate where, the rituals and rules of the synagogue. But inside they were full of jealousy, envy, bitterness, judgmentalism and hate. Jesus stepped on the scene and He does not deny that some of their outward actions are important. But He stresses that to have your religion mean something, you have to start inside. This inward cleansing is what makes the outside truly count for something. Without one, the other becomes vain.

In I Corinthians 6:20, the Apostle Paul commands Christians to *"glorify God in your body, **and in your spirit**."* Once again stressing the need for a person to work on both the outside and ***inside*** of their lives. We must make sure that our inward actions are giving God true glory as much as our outside. Many times we glory in our outward holiness standards while inwardly we are ungodly.

This danger of the concept of taking pride in our outward holiness while neglecting our inward holiness can be seen in the story of Lucifer that we find in Ezekiel 28:12-18. In verses 13 and 14, we learn just how beautiful, talented and special this anointed cherub was. But while he spent a lot of time polishing up that outward appearance, he was neglecting to keep his inward part clean as well. In verse 15, Ezekiel writes, *"Thou wast perfect in thy ways from the day that thou wast created, **till iniquity was found in thee**."* Lucifer was created to reflect the glory and holiness of God, but when he became consumed by his outward appearance of beauty and neglected his inward spirit, he fell. His sin began in the inward part of him and then contaminated the outward. Verse 17 states, *"Thine heart was lifted up because of thy beauty, thou hast corrupted thy wisdom by reason of thy brightness."* In fact the pride he had in his outward beauty caused his inward part to become rotten. We cannot unlink the two parts of us when we are discussing holiness. We must understand the importance of working on ***both*** areas of our lives. But just like any renovation project, where do you start? First you tear down all the rotten things inside so that you can see what needs to be fixed.

In I Thessalonians 5:23, Paul writes, *"...and I pray God your **whole spirit and soul** and body be preserved blameless unto the coming of our Lord Jesus Christ."* Paul reiterates this command of Jesus by desiring that our inward man as well as our outward man be preserved **blameless** (holy) until we could see Jesus again. We must understand the importance of beginning this process on the inside of us. Allow His Spirit to come in daily and commune with our spirit. Then His Spirit leads our spirit to make the right decisions with our soul. This soul then leads our actions on a daily basis to conform to His image and to His holiness.

Inward Holiness

Carla Burton

Chapter 2

Inward Holiness *is Essential for Salvation*

The Holy Ghost Makes Inward Holiness Possible

So how do we obey I Peter 1:16 and the command to *be holy like He is holy*? When we understand that our spirit was separated from God's Spirit through sin, then we need to understand how to rid our lives of that to be able to reconnect to God. So it is through the receiving of the Holy Ghost, the quickening (resurrection) of our spirits, that we are able to have holiness in our inward parts. Remember we must have His Spirit cleansing our spirit so that we can really live a holy life.

When Adam & Eve sinned and evil (sin) invades their thinking, it changes both their inward position before God, but it also changes their outward appearance. They try to cloth themselves, because they see their nakedness in a whole new way. And then they hid themselves (avoid) the presence of God. But before Adam and Eve were cast out of the Garden, we see God teach them the proper way to cover their sins so that they can have limited access back into His presence. Genesis 3:21, *"Unto Adam also and to his wife did the Lord God make **coats of skins, and clothed them**."* To make a coat of skin, you have to take the life of the animal and shed the blood. God teaching them that only the shedding of blood can cover sin, but He didn't stop there. He taught them that their own idea of what was holy for an outward covering was not acceptable to Him. He took the animal that shed it's blood and designed them the first clothing to cover the outward sign of their shameful and sinful behavior. We know that they learned this lesson because we see that they taught their children the correct manner to create an acceptable offering to God. Abel knew and did it correct, while Cain, with a willful nature, did not obey in a manner that was acceptable to God.

Ephesians 2:1-5 tells us that we were dead in our trespasses and sins and that this state controlled our behavior. Verse 3, *"Among whom also we all had our **conversation in times past in the lusts of our flesh, fulfilling the desires of the flesh and of the mind**; and were by nature the children of wrath, even as others."* But then it goes on to tell us in verse 5 that our resurrection (salvation) is found in Christ.

Now do you understand why Jesus tells Nicodemus in John 3 that he must be ***born again***?! Even Nicodemus misunderstood because he was trying to be *physically* reborn. Jesus had to clarify in John 3:5-8, *"Jesus answered, Verily, verily, I say unto thee, Except a man be **born of water and of the Spirit**, he cannot enter into the kingdom of God. That which is born of the flesh is flesh; and that which is born of the Spirit is spirit. Marvel not that I said unto thee, Ye must be born again."* This new birth includes being born again of the water (baptism) and of the Spirit (Holy Ghost). In fact John 6:63 says, *"It is **the spirit that quickeneth**; the flesh profiteth nothing: the words that I speak unto you, they are spirit, and they are life."* It is only through the application of water baptism and the infilling of the Holy Ghost that we can see our spirit man completely resurrected. This then creates a reconnection of our spirit to His Spirit and then we can walk in that.

In Jeremiah 31:31-34 we see a description of the fact that this infilling of the Spirit is going to be written first on the *inward parts of man*. We see this take place on the day of Pentecost in Acts 2:1-4. We see 3 steps of the Spirit of God. First it sat *upon* them, then it *filled* them and the finally they began to *walk* in the Spirit. God's Spirit wrote a new covenant on their hearts. From that day forward we have had the power of God **inwardly** to help us know Him and become like Him. This is the new **birth** experience and the quickening or resurrection of the spirit of man back to the Spirit of God.

This is the first step in Inward Holiness. Without this reconnection of our spirit to God, we will be unable to walk continually in inward holiness.

It's Up to You

While the Holy Ghost makes it possible for us to have inward holiness, it is still our responsibility to enact that power. In Proverbs 20:27, Solomon writes, "The *spirit of man* is the candle of the LORD, searching all the **inward** parts of the belly." Once our spirit has been revived by His Spirit, the Holy Ghost will send light into our lives and help us to clean up our inward man. John 3:21 states, *"But he that doeth truth cometh to the light, that his deeds may be made manifest, that they are wrought in God."* God will help us search and cleanse our inward parts, but first we must allow the Light of the World into our lives to change us.

Our outward appearance, the way we act, the way we look, and the way we speak will reveal what is within us. This is why it is important to make sure the inward part is cleansed and right in the eyes of God -- so that our outward actions can be made manifest. In Mark 7:14-23, Jesus teaches us that *"**All these evil things come from within, and defile the man.**"* I would ask you, "With what are you filling the inward man?" The more you fill the inward part with the Spirit, the Word, and the Truth, the more you can produce holiness outwardly.

Inward Holiness is Essential for Salvation

Hebrews 12:14, *"Follow peace with all men, **and holiness, without which no man shall see the Lord:***" This scripture makes it clear that holiness is a part of this process of salvation. God desires us to continually cleanse ourselves, beginning inwardly and moving outwardly, because without our conformation to His character (holiness), we cannot see Him. Paul teaches in II Corinthians 4:16, *"For which cause we faint not; but though our outward man perish, yet the **inward** man is renewed day by day."* It is our responsibility to cleanse ourselves each day. Paul saw his need to die daily so that Christ could be glorified through him. God's mercy is new every morning, so all we need to do is ask His forgiveness and He will cleanse us.

Carla Burton

Chapter 3

Inward Holiness *Standards*

Now that we understand this process and recognize the importance of beginning this journey inwardly, let's study *inward holiness standards* and how we can apply them to our lives.

Clean Heart, Right Spirit

II Corinthians 7:1 tells us to cleanse ourselves from all *"filthiness of the spirit."* Remember that a person's inward condition will produce outward fruits, so keeping a right spirit should be the first line of defense for a Christian. If your inward spirit is subjected to the Spirit of God, He will lead you and guide you into outward holiness (as discussed above). Many Christians have great outward holiness standards, but their inward parts are filthy in the sight of God. According to the Word of God, their holiness is in vain and eventually those inward sins are going to show up outwardly.

I want to make sure that we don't glory in one area of our personal holiness standards and neglect the other areas. There are many who think what you do inwardly is the *only* thing that counts, while others live outwardly holy but inwardly they are full of sin and deceit. Once again, recognize that Jesus placed emphasis on **both** areas but He directed us to start this process from within ourselves. I would go one step further and say that once you have cleansed yourself inwardly, you will have to go back again and again to be sure that your inward man stays clean. This is called sanctification and it means to be *"consistently cleansed"*. Just as a person baths each day for bodily cleanliness, the soul must have a cleansing as well. Jesus told us to get up and make sure we *die* or cleanse our flesh so that our spiritual man can thrive.

We may think that we know ourselves completely, but the Word shows us that there are things within us that we cannot even know or understand. We must make sure that we are cleansed from inward sins. Psalm 19:12 sets an example of prayer that we should follow: *"Who can understand his errors?* **cleanse** *thou me from* **secret faults***."* Jesus Himself taught us through the pattern of The Lord's Prayer found in Matthew 6 that we should seek to cleanse ourselves from issues that begin inwardly. *"And lead us not into* **temptation***, but deliver us from evil:"* He knew that as long as our flesh is alive on this earth, there will be a constant struggle to stay purified and acceptable in the sight of God.

David understood that sin started within, and he asked God to cleanse him from within. In Psalm 51:2, he prays, *"Wash me thoroughly from mine iniquity, and cleanse me from my sin."* And he goes on in Psalm 51:10 to say: *"Create in me a* **clean heart***, O God; and* **renew a right spirit within me***."* David mentions his *heart* and his *spirit* as two different things. He is speaking of his *soul* (heart) and his *spirit*. He realizes that because he has not kept his spirit connect to God and clean, it caused his soul to preform and outward actions which had brought sin into his life. There is power when a Christian prays the actual scriptures of the Bible. And there is no more powerful repentance prayer, than Psalm 51. If you feel that you are allowing your spirit to be tainted by this world and then your soul (your actions) are causing you to outwardly sin, then take out your Bible and open it and begin to pray this setting of scripture. As you pray this prayer, do not think about David writing these words about his life, but instead replace him with yourself. Imagine, as you speak each word, that you are speaking to God and asking these things for yourself. If you do this, I know you will begin to feel the weight of those inward sins release from your life. Then your outward man will feel the power to overcome temptation.

In the Old Testament, God spoke through the prophet Ezekiel about something that would happen that would change our hearts and spirits. Remember in the last chapter of this booklet, we discussed the breach that had occurred between us and God through the events that took place in the Garden of Eden. But here in Ezekiel 36:25-27, we see the prophetic utterance of a time when that breach would be healed or reconciled. *"Then will I sprinkle clean water upon you, and ye shall be clean: from all your filthiness, and from all your idols, will I cleanse you.* **A new heart also will I give you, and a new spirit will I put within you***: and I will take away the stony heart out of your flesh, and I will give you an heart of flesh.* **And I will put my spirit within you, and cause you to walk in my statutes, and ye shall keep my judgments, and do them***"* God tells us that the power to keep His judgments and statues only comes from **His Spirit** coming inside of us. His Spirit was poured out in Acts 2 and it filled the heart of all those in that room. There was a reviving of their spirit man to a closeness with the Spirit of God. And through this process they have an ability now that they had never had before to avoid temptation and sin. Then how much more today is it important to maintain a clean heart and a right spirit? We live in a evil world. Jesus told us that it was going to get worse and worse and become like it was in the days of Noah. If we are going to avoid the pitfalls of temptation, then it will only come through keeping our hearts and spirits clean and connect to Almighty God. I encourage you to stop right here and take a moment and ask God to cleanse your heart and spirit one more time.

The more we cleanse ourselves within, the more access to God's presence we have. Remember He is a Holy God and cannot fellowship with sin. That is why we are called to become like Him and be holy so that He can then reconnect in communication with us. James 4:8 states, *"Draw nigh to God, and he will draw nigh to you.* **Cleanse** *your hands, ye sinners; and* **purify your hearts***, ye double minded."* Remember that very root and reason for holiness is to be *pleasing to God and accepted into His presence*. If He cannot dwell with sin, then we must purify our hearts and spirits to maintain access and connection to His Holy Spirit.

So the way we cleanse our spirit is through repentance and the forgiveness of sins. *"But if we walk in the light, as he is in the light, we have fellowship one with another,* **and the blood of Jesus Christ his Son cleanseth us from all sin.** *If we say that we have no sin, we deceive ourselves, and the truth is not in us. If we confess our sins, he is faithful and just to forgive us our sins,* **and to cleanse us from all unrighteousness.***"* (I John 1:7-9) To keep a clean heart and a right spirit is going to take a daily repentance a constant infilling of His Spirit.

A Renewed Mind

Proverbs 23:7 tells us the power of the mind when it says, *"For as he thinketh in his heart, so is he:"* The power of any dream or action begins as a tiny seed of thought in the mind. Today, we answer and hear a voice through a telephone because someone had a thought that it could happen. We fly on planes because someone *thought* that it was possible. There is immense power in our thoughts.

Satan was perfect until that one thought took root that he should be equal with God. Adam and Eve had a perfect life until Eve had a conversation with a serpent and a thought took root in her mind. Cain killed his own brother because a thought produced a feeling which resulted in an action.

God spoke to Solomon concerning having a "willing" or renewed mind in I Chronicles 28:9, *"And thou, Solomon my son, know thou the God of thy father, and serve him with **a perfect heart and with a willing mind**: for the Lord searcheth all hearts, and understandeth all the imaginations of the thoughts: if thou seek him, he will be found of thee; but if thou forsake him, he will cast thee off for ever."* He showed Solomon that the key to being accepted into His presence was knowing Him and seeking Him with a perfect heart and a willing (or renewed) mind. Our minds are where the battle for our souls begins, and when we are born again, we become a new creature in Christ. However, the battle for our minds continues daily. Satan uses every tool he has available to win this battle, so it takes an effort and agreement with God to stay in a renewed mind on a daily basis.

Pastors and teachers must understand that our job is to change *minds*, not hearts. Only God has the power to change a heart! But our responsibility is to continually teach the Word of God so that knowledge can increase. Teaching the Word of God instills truth in the mind of the student, and then their heart will surely follow. Many times we try to change hearts, which people may resist because they don't have a foundation of knowledge on which to base the change in their lives. I encourage you to stop for a moment and read Proverbs 2. Solomon, the wisest man who ever lived, gives us an insight into just how powerful it is to gain knowledge and wisdom. He says in verse 10-11, *"When wisdom entereth into thine heart, and knowledge is pleasant unto thy soul; Discretion shall preserve thee, understanding shall keep thee:"* And when these two things from God take over your mind, you can maintain integrity inwardly which will produce outward results. But this all starts in the *mind*.

How do you renew the mind? I would like to be able to give you some new and exciting way to do this. But, in truth, the same pattern that the Christian much institute in every other area of their lives, is still the only way when it comes to renewing the mind. And that is connecting your mind to God through the reading of the Word, prayer and worship! A renewed mind is simply based on *what you feed it everyday!* Look at what it says in I Peter 1:13-16 (Easy To Read Version), *"**So prepare your minds** for service. With complete self-control put all your hope in the grace that will be yours when Jesus Christ comes. In the past you did not have the understanding you have now, so you did the evil things you wanted to do. But now you are children of God, so you should obey him and not live the way you did before. Be holy in everything you do, just as God is holy. He is the one who chose you. In the Scriptures God says, "Be holy, because I am holy."* We prepare (renew) our minds through self-control. We get up each day and make a choice to set boundaries around our mind. We have been given the knowledge and we have been given the infilling of His Spirit to help us take charge of our minds.

The Apostle Paul understood this immense battle that took place in our lives between good and evil. He relates this to us in Romans 7:14-25. He illuminates how hard this daily struggle of renewing the mind is. He winds it all up in verse 22-27 by saying this, *"For I delight in the law of God after the inward man: **But I see another law in my members, warring against the law of my mind**, and bringing me into captivity to the law of sin which is in* *my members. O wretched man that I am! who shall deliver me from the body of this death? I thank God through Jesus Christ our Lord.* **So then with the mind I myself serve the law of God**; *but with the flesh the law of sin."* The true relationship with God begins in this battlefield called our mind. But we can bring our mind into subjection by *daily* washing our minds with the Word of God and prayer. This then produces a *renewed mind*.

Jesus said that the greatest commandment of all is for a person to love God with all his or her mind (Matthew 22:37). There is a saying that if you live for God easy, it is hard; but if you live for God hard, it is easy. We must make sure that our minds are committed to Christ first, and then our bodies will follow. When you love God with everything you are, then there is no room left over to give to other things. Christ-centered lives are truly holy lives.

The Benefits of a Renewed Mind

So now we understand that renewed mind keeps us connect to God on a daily basis. But there are some additional benefits released to us when we take control and live with a renewed mind.

A renewed mind brings peace to a life. In Isaiah 26:3, the prophet states, *"Thou wilt keep him in perfect peace, whose* **mind** *is stayed on thee: because he trusteth in thee."* A mind that is *stayed or renewed* on God is a person who truly knows peace no matter their circumstance. When someone has a peaceful mind (inward holiness), then they will produce peace (outward holiness). If a person's mind is renewed in Christ, that person will produce peace personally and then peace in the home and peace in the church. Many churches suffer continually with church problems because the church members do not have renewed minds; they are carnally minded. They have not taken the time or effort to renew their minds and so what they are allowing to take place inwardly will always show up outwardly. Romans 8:6-7 states, *"For to be* *carnally minded is death; but to be **spiritually minded is life and peace**. Because the carnal **mind** is enmity against God: for it is not subject to the law of God, neither indeed can be."* A carnal mind is the opposite of a renewed mind, and we see in the scripture setting above that we get a carnal mind by *not* subjecting ourselves to the law of God (the Bible)! We must keep our minds centered on God and His Word and be filled with His Spirit. If we do our part, He has promised us life and peace.

Another benefit of a renewed mind is the ability to have a complete transformation in your life. The very root of holiness is transformation of both mind and body to be like Christ. In Romans 12:1-2, we see where this transformation truly begins. *" I beseech you therefore, brethren, by the mercies of God, that ye **present your bodies a living sacrifice, holy, acceptable unto God**, which is your reasonable service. And be not conformed to this world: but be ye **transformed by the renewing of your mind**, that ye may prove what is that good, and acceptable, and perfect, will of God."* When you allow your mind to be renewed, then the rest of your body will be transformed as well. What you think is what you become. This is the power that is found in the *mind*. Reading the Word of God shows us how to live, praying helps us to agree with God, and walking in the Spirit produces holiness in our lives. Once the battle for your mind is won, you can then begin living a new life of righteousness and "true" holiness according to Ephesians 4:21-24. *"If so be that ye have heard him, and have been taught by him, as the truth is in Jesus: That ye put off concerning the former conversation the old man, which is corrupt according to the deceitful lusts; And be **renewed in the spirit of your mind**; And that ye put on the new man, which after God is created in righteousness and true holiness."* The true power of this transformation begin when we allow our minds to be changed first! He goes in Ephesians 4:25-32 to show us how we can then act and treat others but we will never be able to do these things unless we win the battle in our minds first.

One of the final benefits of a renewed mind is that we can actually not just resist evil but we can actually begin to take on the mind of Christ. I Corinthians 2:16: *"For who hath known the mind of the Lord, that he may instruct him? But we have the **mind** of Christ."* Philippians 2:5: *"Let this **mind** be in you, which was also in Christ Jesus."* When you allow His Spirit to come into your life and bring knowledge and wisdom, and then you daily renew your mind through prayer and the washing of the Word of God, then your perspective will change. You will begin to think like Christ thinks. And this is *true holiness*, which means conforming to His character and likeness. How powerful to be able to say that your mind has been so renewed or transformed that you think like Jesus.

Keeping our minds renewed *daily* is one of the greatest inward holiness standards that we can accomplish. And it is one of the biggest battles that we **must** win if we are going to be a transformed, holy Christian.

The Works of the Flesh

We are working our way through these inward holiness issues that we must conqueror *first*. As we conqueror these issues inwardly, there will be outward fruit produced. So don't skim through these issues and try to work from the outside back inward. Take the time, make the effort, absorb the knowledge and then let your obedience follow. Plant the seed and let it grow before trying to eat the fruit of it.

You may look at the works of the flesh and ask why these are not included in the booklet on outward holiness? But as we begin to read through these and study them, you will realize that all these *works* of the flesh begin with a thought. And then that thought is germinated in our lives until our hearts and spirits are unclean. And then our outward action will always follow what is within us. So to make sure that we are not doing the works of the flesh, we have to begin the work by defining what they are and cut them off at the root (inwardly).

Galatians 5:19-21 gives us the list of the works of the flesh. *"Now the works of the flesh are manifest, which are these; Adultery, fornication, uncleanness, lasciviousness, Idolatry, witchcraft, hatred, variance, emulations, wrath, strife, seditions, heresies, Envyings, murders, drunkenness, revellings, and such like: of the which I tell you before, as I have also told you in time past, that they which do such things shall not inherit the kingdom of God."* The Christian has to be careful, when reading this list, that they do not focus only on the ones they are successfully shunning and pass over the ones that they have issues with. Many Christians can say they would never be an adulterer, a fornicator, involved in witchcraft or drunken; however, they overlook the smaller works of the flesh. They can be foolish in their behavior, constantly in variance or conflict with one another, not submitted to the authority in their lives, or emulating the stature of pastor or teacher. I think we must take another look at this scripture and make sure that our outward holiness is reflecting a true inward holiness.

So to make sure that we are shunning *all* the works of the flesh let's define some of the ones that may be a little harder to understand. The first one we come to that we may not fully understand is *uncleanness*. This has nothing to do with personal hygiene, but the definition means to be immoral or indecent. To be immoral means that you know what is moral and right but you make a conscious choice to do what is wrong. It is when you know that something is the right or decent thing to do but you chose to do what is wrong or indecent. If you know it is wrong to steal but you choose to do it, you are immoral and indecent. If you know you should not lie or mistreat others, but you make a conscious choice to commit this behavior, you are immoral or indecent. Paul talking to the **church** at Corinth said in II Corinthians 12:21, *"And lest, when I come again, my God will humble me among you, and that I shall bewail many which have sinned already, and have not repented of the uncleanness and fornication and lasciviousness which they have committed."* I want you to make the correlation that he is speaking to *church people* about the works of the flesh that they were allowing to reign in their lives. He mentions uncleanness and indicated that they were doing the opposite of what they knew was right to do.

And again in I Thessalonians 4:1-7, Paul emphasizes the importance of doing what you know is right! *"Furthermore then we beseech you, brethren, and exhort you by the Lord Jesus, that as ye have received of us **how ye ought to walk and to please God**, so ye would abound more and more. For ye know what commandments we gave you by the Lord Jesus. For this is the will of God, even your sanctification, that ye should abstain from fornication: **That every one of you should know how** to possess his vessel in sanctification and honour; Not in the lust of concupiscence, even as the Gentiles which know not God: That no man go beyond and defraud his brother in any matter: because that the Lord is the avenger of all such, as we also have forewarned you and testified. **For God hath not called us unto uncleanness, but unto holiness.**"* Paul is making the point to these Christians that they *know what is right to do* and therefore they are responsible to abstain from choosing to do the opposite. When you are unclean, you are someone who makes a knowing choice to do the opposite of what is right.

Then we come to that big word, *lasciviousness*. The means to have vices and in particular sexual vices. It is unbridled lust that leads to sinful behavior. When we study the story of Sodom and

Gomorrah, we see the reign of lasciviousness in their lives. They were so sexually deviant that they would come to someone's home in the middle of the night and seek to defile them. When we allow ourselves to view pornography, in any form, then we have allowed this work of the flesh to begin in our lives.

As Christians, we need to carefully and honestly check our lives when it comes to the topic of pornography. We may not have the hardest types of pornography in our lives but we have to guard against books we read, magazines we look at it, movies and TV that we watch, even commercials that we allow our eyes to view. The world is going to grow worse and worse. We cannot allow them to set the line for us in regards to what is pornographic. We have to be sure that we, the Christian, are filtering what we allow into our lives through God's guidelines. As the world becomes the anti-Christ in their beliefs and boundaries, we must become more *Christ like* in our minds and actions. That is the only way that we can combat against this work of the flesh called lasciviousness. And we must be prepared because the world will mock us for our views. Our Vice-President, Mike Pence, has made a commitment that he will not have a meal with another woman without his wife present. He is making a conscious choice to avoid lasciviousness in his life. He is not leaving a door open for this work of the flesh to take root. And he is mocked because of this behavior. While the world continues the sexualization of young girls and teenagers which has released an epidemic of sexual abuse, harassment and deviant behavior towards women. The challenge for the Christian today is to go through our lives and clean out those things that would lead us into lasciviousness.

The next word in Galatians 5 that may be hard for us to understand is *variance*. Variance means to have discord, conflict, dissension and contention with someone or something to the point that you cannot control yourself. And that this causes a split or separation between you and that other thing. I use the word *thing* because this does not just apply to our relationship with other people. But it can also apply to our relationship with the Word of God and obedience to what it tells us. It definitely applies to your relationship with God!

You must understand that even in the *church* there are those that are variant. They look for every opportunity to cause division and discord. Many of them even let you know up front whose team they are on, they call themselves the *devil's advocates!!* They have one goal; to create conflict, confusion, anger, discord and disunity among the body of Christ. They may not even realize what spirit has attached itself to them and is ruling their lives. But, we must be careful that we don't allow this work of the flesh to attach itself to us.

Paul taught us in Romans 16:17-18 that we have to mark these people and avoid them. *"Now I beseech you, brethren,* **mark them which cause divisions and offences contrary to the doctrine which ye have learned; and avoid them**. *For they that are such serve not our Lord Jesus Christ, but their own belly; and by good words and fair speeches deceive the hearts of the simple."* We have two responsibilities when it comes to variance. First, we must make sure we are not the person who has this spirit in our lives. We need to watch negativity to vision, disagreement with the Word or the man of God and the tendency to walk around angry or embittered. We are the only person who can fix ourselves. Make sure that you are not producing the work of the flesh called variance in your own life. Then secondly, avoid hanging around with people who exhibit this type of behavior. Take an honest look at your circle of *friends* in the church. What type of conversations do you have? Are they consistently negative and disruptive? Does your group always tear down any new idea presented by the church or the Pastor? Do they rip apart messages preached from the pulpit and try to share their personal opinions? If you have that type of friend, then you need to begin to break that relationship and avoid them, especially if you want to change your behavior. The Bible teaches us that "like spirits are drawn to like spirits", so change your group and you can begin to change your spirit.

Jesus never had deep conversations with the Pharisees because they only approached Him with a spirit of variance. In fact, when Jesus did answer them it was very harsh and cutting. Several times he called them out as snakes (vipers) and hypocrites. Many Christians today would never survive us calling them out on their behavior with such words. But it's still true today that if your approach to God, His Word, your Pastor, his vision and your church is always negative, then you need to check your spirit for variance.

The Bible clearly tells us the power that is found in unity. Variance is the complete opposite of unity and therefore probably the most successful tool that Satan uses to destroy a church from within. When we receive the Holy Ghost in our lives, we get the fruit of the spirit. One of the fruit we receive is *temperance* which is defined as self-control. We *do* have the ability, with God's help, to control ourselves when it comes to variance (discord). So take an honest look at your life and make sure that this work of the flesh is not ruling you.

Then we see the word *emulations* which mean to have an envious rivalry; or to have so much ambition that you desire to be equal or excel others. This word finds it's root all the way back to before the creation of the world. Isaiah 14:12-14 gives us insight into the emulations that Lucifer had towards God. *"How art thou fallen from heaven, O Lucifer, son of the morning! how art thou cut down to the ground, which didst weaken the nations! For thou hast said in thine heart,* ***I will ascend into heaven, I will exalt my throne above the stars of God: I will sit also upon the mount of the congregation, in the sides of the north: I will ascend above***

the heights of the clouds; I will be like the most High." Satan began to desire to emulate God, His power and His position. We look at this example and see it as extreme behavior and something that we would never do. Yet each week, *Christians* speak about their Pastor or even God like this. Their words and actions tell the story that they feel they are equal in authority to both. We have to be careful that we don't allow this work of the flesh that destroyed Satan to become our destruction as well.

Today's environment of social media has also exponentially increased the spirit of emulations, especially in the church world. Multiple times each day, people are posting and tweeting about *their victories*. Others read through these and a spirit of envy begins to rise in them. What is the answer? Maybe one way is to work harder at making sure our posts lift up Jesus and not just exalt what is happening to us personally. We have to be careful that we don't fall into the same trap that Satan set for Eve, when he told her that if she ate the fruit she would *be like god*! He caught her in the web of emulation and she took the bait. Be careful with your social media. If you find that you cannot look at social media without an envious spirit rising up inside of you, then cut it out of your life.

The opposite of emulation is to be submitted. When we submit one to another, we actually destroy this work of the flesh. We need to watch our spirits and make sure that we are defeating the work of emulations by submitting wholeheartedly to God, His Word, our Pastor's and leaders as well as even to others around us. Going to someone and submitting yourself to them in word and deed can destroy the bait of emulation.

The next work of the flesh that gives us trouble is the word sedition. This mean overt conduct, either in speech or organization, that leads to insurrection (rebellion) against authority. The difference between variance and sedition is that variance is creating conflict due to a lack of control of your temper, but sedition is actually plotting and organizing an uprising against the spiritual authority in your life. This is an extremely dangerous work of the flesh. It is the closest in action to what Lucifer did when he persuaded 1/3 of the angels in heaven to rebel against God with him.

In Exodus 32, the Children of Israel are encamped around the base of Mt. Sinai waiting on Moses to come down from his meeting with God. The get tired of waiting and they begin a sedition against God and the man of God, Moses. They convince Aaron to build them a golden calf and then they are going to return to Egypt.

Sedition is the completed fruit from the seed of variance. Often we will see someone who cannot control themselves and becomes so bitter and angry that they begin to spread discord. As this variance goes unchecked it leads to sedition, where the person will work to get others to see their point of view and they create an organized rebellion against leadership and authority.

We must understand that God hates sedition, because He knows it is the actions of a stubborn, stiff-necked, unrepentant heart. It is during the time of variance that God extends mercy and is long suffering with us to get ourselves right. But it is different with sedition. By the time you reach this place of seditious behavior, you have allowed the work of variance to rule your life. So when the culmination of that fruit is sedition, God's only answer to that is swift and final judgment. We get a little insight to how swift and final that judgment can be in Luke 10:18, *"And he said unto them, I beheld Satan as lightning fall from heaven."* God's judgment on Satan's seditious behavior was fast and final.

We cannot allow ourselves to produce the work of sedition in our lives. The key to overcoming this, is to take care of our issues of variance. And be careful that you are not allowing ourselves to be swept up in someone else's seditious behavior. Proverbs 6:16-19 tells us that there are 7 things the Lord hates and men that sow discord among their brethren is on that list. This is sedition, when you would take your issue and begin to infect a congregation with it with the purpose of dividing the people. Don't allow a seditious spirit to infect your life and don't allow yourself around those type of people.

Then we come to the word heresies. A heresy is an opinion, doctrine, or practice *contrary to the truth* or to generally accepted beliefs or standards. This is when someone causes confusion about the truth that they have been given or taught. It is when they have essentially embraced false doctrine. The apostle Paul in Galatians 1:6-9 reiterates this to the church at Galatia when he says, *"I marvel that ye are so soon removed from him that called you into the grace of Christ* **unto another gospel.** *Which is not another; but there be some that trouble you,* **and would pervert the gospel of Christ. But though we, or an angel from heaven, preach any other gospel unto you than that which we have preached unto you, let him be accursed.** *As we said before, so say I now again,* **if any man preach any other gospel unto you than that ye have received, let him be accursed.***"* Paul tells us that even if an angel comes down from heaven with another doctrine besides what you have already been given, we need to reject that and hold fast to what we have already received. This is the importance of reading and knowing the Word of God, of understanding the truth of sound doctrine. We must make sure that our doctrine and the things we would hear line up to the Word of God. I Timothy 4:1-2 says, *"Now the Spirit speaketh expressly, that in the latter times some shall depart from the faith, giving heed to seducing spirits, and doctrines of devils; Speaking lies in hypocrisy; having their conscience seared with a hot iron;"* These people are in the world today. They read the same Scriptures you and I read, but they twist what they hear to line up with ***their own belief system.*** They don't allow the Word to change them, but rather they try and change the Word to fit their life. Paul understood how important it was for Timothy to hold fast to the sound doctrine that he had been given. He wanted him to know that in the last days people were going to grow worse and worse. In fact they were going to be so twisted in their doctrine they were going to look for a man of God who would agree with them, and they would find one. 2 Timothy 4:3-4, *"For the time will come when they will not endure sound doctrine; but after their own lusts shall they heap to themselves teachers, having itching ears; And they shall turn away their ears from the truth, and shall be turned unto fables."*

Our doctrine is built upon the Word of God. We built our salvation plan upon the words of Jesus Christ and the apostle's doctrine. We read the Word and instead of trying to twist the Word to fit our lives, we change to mirror what His Word says. When you understand the Word and receive an illumination of what is being spoken, then hold fast to that. Don't allow yourself to be draw into a heresy with someone. Don't try and change the Word for your comfort. Instead, hold fast to sound doctrine and walk in it daily.

And the final word that we often overlook in this scripture regarding shunning the works of the flesh is *revelries*. This word means foolishness or carousing. Ephesians 5:4, *"Neither filthiness, nor **foolish talking**, **nor jesting**, which are not convenient: but rather giving of thanks."* He was speaking to the saints and instructing them in the things we should avoid. This seems to be a small work of the flesh, but more people have gotten trip up by this *small fox* more than any other. Being foolish and allowing revelries to overtake us can lead us into a path that will destroy our lives.

The prodigal son walked down this path when he took his inheritance and left home. In fact Luke 15 records his actions as one who traveled into a far land *and there wasted his substance with riotous living.* He spent all that he had on revelries and foolish living.

We live in a generation that is addicted to pleasure. Our minds are consumed with what gives us joy, what we can relax and do, what gives us pleasure. But the Word tells us that these worldly pleasures only give temporary relief. This was what the prodigal son also learned. When all the money was gone and the fun was no longer an option, he realized that all the *fun* hadn't really been that fun. You see there is only true, complete satisfaction in filling that empty place inside of you with the presence of God. Your inward man was created to be filled by God and no matter how many pleasures and distractions you throw at it, the hole in your life will never be filled. It's like a black hole in space, it will keep sucking the pleasures in but never be full. The only way you can truly fill that place is to turn to God, His Word, His Presence and His will for your life. When you surrender to God, there is a peace and contentment that comes upon you. Then you won't have to seek out the foolish things of this world to try and find rest. Be careful that you don't allow yourself to get caught up in revelries because they can ultimate destroy your life.

The ability to shun the works of the flesh, these outward actions, really begins within us. Jesus lets us know that all these outward signs start inwardly. He says in Matthew 5:28, *"But I say unto you, That whosoever looketh on a woman to lust after her hath committed adultery with her already in his heart."* In I John 3:15, He says, *"Whosoever hateth his brother is a murderer...."* Many people say that living under the Old Testament law would have been easier, but Jesus dispels that notion in the scriptures above. In the Old Testament you had to be found in the act of adultery to be punished, and you had to have actually killed someone to be a murderer. In the New Testament, Jesus shows us that the mind is where the sin begins. If you lust after a woman (an inward thought), in His eyes you have already committed adultery. If you hate your brother (an inward emotion), you have already committed murder in God's eyes. This scripture shows us the importance of keeping an inwardly clean spirit, mind, and heart so that we can be holy in God's sight.

Mark 7:18-22, *"And he saith unto them, Are ye so without understanding also? Do ye not perceive, that whatsoever thing from without entereth into the man, it cannot defile him; Because it entereth not into his heart, but into the belly, and goeth out into the draught, purging all meats? And he said, That which cometh out of the man, that defileth the man.* ***For from within, out of the heart of men****, proceed evil thoughts, adulteries, fornications, murders, Thefts, covetousness, wickedness, deceit, lasciviousness, an evil eye, blasphemy, pride, foolishness:* ***All these evil things come from within, and defile the man.****"*

Study the works of the flesh. Know and understand what each of them mean and then spend time honestly looking at your life, your actions. Allow God's Spirit to help you overcome the works of the flesh so that you can live free and blessed.

Guard Your Tongue

A large part of holiness is guarding the tongue. When we allow our tongue to control us, then we will always wind up in trouble. It is hard work for a person to guard his tongue, but until a person can control it, that person cannot live in true holiness.

We are instructed in Psalm 34:13 to *"Keep thy tongue from evil, and thy lips from speaking guile."* This scripture lets you know it is your responsibility to control your tongue. It says, "Keep thy"! It's *your* job is to control what comes out of your mouth.

I Peter 3:10 states, *"For he that will love life, and see good days, let him refrain his tongue from evil, and his lips that they speak no guile....*" If you want peace and happiness, you will learn early on to control what comes from your mouth. I have a personal mantra: If you know someone is talking about me, DON'T TELL ME! If I know, then I will have to pray through it and forgive them. I want a life of peace and joy and I want to greet my brothers and sisters without any restraint from my heart, so I do two things: I watch what I say, and I don't listen to negative talk from others.

Proverbs 18:21 states, *"Death and life are in the power of the tongue: and they that love it shall eat the fruit thereof."* If you find someone who loves to "talk" about others, AVOID THIS PERSON! If you learn to love the taste of that fruit you will find that one day you have to eat it also! You have the power to build someone up or to destroy someone by what you say. And if you use your tongue to produce life, then you will eat the fruit of good things and life affirming things spoken to you and about you as well.

The problem is that we get in a situation where we learn that we are being spoken of in a negative fashion and our immediate response is to retaliate. This is the opposite of what Jesus taught us. He told us to turn the other cheek, and to forgive. He also taught us that if there is vengeance that needs to take place, it would come from Him. The military has a phrase called *collateral damage.* When they are going to drop a bomb in a certain location, they always assess what is close to the impact site. They will look for schools, hospitals and homes. Because innocent people killed during a bombing event are called collateral damage and the military works hard to keep that number down. In fact, they have often called off a bombing due to the fact that there would be too many innocent people caught in the crossfire. I believe that the God's vengeance and judgment is the same. There are many times that God would like to take care of a someone that has been speaking against you. But because your are still too close to the situation, God cannot implement His plan because you may become collateral damage. If someone has hurt or wounded you with their tongue, don't respond in kind. Don't try and defend yourself. Don't worry about getting back at them. Instead, pray for them and remove yourself from their sphere as quickly as possible. This allows God the ability to measure to them the fruit of what they have been speaking without hurting or damaging you in anyway.

James 1:26 teaches us, *"If any man among you seem to be religious, and bridleth not his tongue, but deceiveth his own heart, this man's religion is vain."* Don't be deceived; just because everyone attends church doesn't mean they are in church. Don't be too upset when your "brothers" talk about you; remember that some people's religion is vain, according to the Word of God. You can tell these people by the ones who can't control their tongues.

"Even so the tongue is a little member, and boasteth great things. Behold, how great a matter a little fire kindleth! ***And the tongue is a fire, a world of iniquity: so is the tongue among our members, that it defileth the whole body,*** *and setteth on fire the course of nature; and it is set on fire of hell…. But the tongue can no man tame; it is an unruly evil, full of deadly poison."* (James 3:5-6, 8) We must realize that our tongues can be full of evil and the only way to keep them under control is to subject them to Spirit of God. Keeping our spirits and hearts subject to Him, and our lives full of the Holy Ghost can help us to keep our tongues from destroying us. If you are using your mouth to praise God you shouldn't have time to destroy others.

And as a member of your local church, you should understand your role for the Pastor is to be a fireman, not an arsonist! When you are a part of a conversation that is not right, you can either pour water or gasoline on it. Your pastor needs you to pour water and put out those fires before they get out of control. By learning to separate yourself from people who talk, you will find they don't come to you anymore and this will bring great joy and peace to your life. So make guarding your tongue a key ingredient in your Inward Holiness process.

Abstain from the Appearance of Evil

I Thessalonians 5:22 admonishes us to *"Abstain from all appearance of evil. And the very God of peace sanctify you wholly; and I pray God your whole spirit and soul and body be preserved blameless unto the coming of our Lord Jesus Christ."*

This word abstain means to hold oneself back voluntarily, especially from something regarded as improper or unhealthy. This is a voluntary action, something you ***chose*** to not participate in. There are many activities I could do that wouldn't be sin; but I chose to not participate in them. The reason that I make this choice is so that I can keep myself from even the appearance of evil. Does this mean that I am being fake? No, it means that I am choosing not to commit an act that may hinder my witness before others. When I profess that I am a believer and follower of Jesus Christ, it may call for me to modify my behavior when it could be confusing to others. My witness is more important to me than participating in something that may only give me a temporary pleasure.

Many people don't want to apply this scripture to their lives and they will use the excuse about something they want to participate in by saying, "This is not a heaven or hell issue". If that is the excuse that you use to keep from submitting your life to this scripture then you are missing the whole point of holiness. This is not about what I can get away with, but it's about what I can do to become more like Him and more pleasing to Him! When I weigh the value of my reputation against an activity, I quickly realize that

I desire for people to respect that I belong to God more. Shunning the appearance of evil means protecting your witness more than anything else in the world. This battle will always begin in your mind and heart and then be relayed outwardly in your actions. So honestly look at your life and your actions and shun the appearance of evil.

Carla Burton

Chapter 4

Fruits of Inward Holiness

Fruits of the Spirit

It's not enough to just shun the works of the flesh, guarding your tongue, and avoiding the appearance of evil. You must be actively producing the fruit of the Spirit described in Galatians 5:22-24. I have often asked people, "What are you promoting in your church?" Is it love, joy, and peace? Are you longsuffering towards your brothers and sisters? Are you meek? Do you produce faith? Many people will tell you they don't sin by committing the works of the flesh, but they also are not producing inward holiness through the fruit of the Spirit.

Paul says in Ephesians 5:9-10, *"(For the **fruit** of the Spirit is in all goodness and righteousness and truth;)* **Proving what is acceptable unto the Lord.***"* Remember holiness is about being acceptable to God, and this scripture lets us know that producing the fruit of the Spirit is one step in the right direction.

Unity & Love for One Another

One of the greatest witnesses of holiness is unity among the brethren. And yet, unity is one of the greatest problems in our local churches. We say we are Christians, yet we devour one another. Many Christians need to take a moment and look within themselves and really gain a love for one another. We have the ability to increase in our love for one another according to I Thessalonians 3:12-13, *"And the Lord make you to **increase and abound in love one toward another**, and toward all men, even as we do toward you: To the end **he may stablish your hearts unblameable in holiness before God**, even our Father, at the coming of our Lord Jesus Christ with all his saints."* I John 4:7-12, 20-21)

Many people in our churches today don't understand why their prayers go unanswered or why they don't even feel confident when they pray and ask God for something. I John 3:11-23 gives us some insight into the reason why and I encourage you to read the entire portion of scripture. In verse 18-22 he tells us, *"My little children, let us not love in word, neither in tongue; but in deed and in truth. And hereby we know that we are of the truth, and **shall assure our hearts before him. For if our heart condemn us**, God is greater than our heart, and knoweth all things. **Beloved, if our heart condemn us not, then have we confidence toward God. And whatsoever we ask, we receive of him, because we keep his commandments, and do those things that are pleasing in his sight.**"* This is in a scripture setting where he is discussing the fact that we, the children of God, should manifest our love for one another. If you have something against your brother or have mistreated them, then it's going to be hard to go before God and sincerely ask something of Him. Your heart will condemn you which will cause you to not have the confidence to seek your answer from Him. And all this stems from the fact that we are not following the commandment of God in our lives to love one another and treat each other with respect.

The love that we have for our brothers and sisters in Christ is key to our ability to seek God in prayer and receive and answer. But love and unity is not just for receiving what we need, it is also a part of our witness to others. *"A new commandment I give unto you, That ye love one another; as I have loved you, that ye also love one another. By this shall all men know that ye are my disciples, if ye have love one to another."* Others will understand God's love by how we show our love for one another. They will understand that we are truly a disciple of Christ when we love one another and create a spirit of unity. A large part of holiness is creating unity in our churches by loving, caring, praying, and ministering to one another.

There is no greater love manifested, in the eyes of God, than a person loving his or her neighbor. In John 15:12-13, Jesus tells us that we truly know love when we are willing to deny ourselves, or "die" to the flesh, so that someone else can be saved. Sometimes we are talked about, mistreated, and abused by the very people who are supposed to support us in love; however, a true, holy Christian is one who sees the greater purpose in the Kingdom of God and holds his tongue. Remember that God said He rewards all vengeance (Romans 12:19). We need to withhold our personal issues and love one another so that unity will not be destroyed.

Many people think that loving one another is a choice, but Christ *"commands"* us to love one another. He says, *"These things I command you, that ye **love one another**."* (John 15:17) This is your scripture for those people who are often difficult to love; just remember that Christ commands us to love one another. And in I John 4:7-12; 20-21 we see that we cannot say we love God and hate our brother. God is love and if we really belong to

Him, then that will include loving our brothers in Christ, even the difficult ones.

You will know that you have true unity in love when you are unselfish in your dealings with your spiritual brethren. Paul reminds us in Romans 12:10 to *"Be kindly affected one to another with **brotherly love**; in honour preferring one another...."* And in II Corinthians 2:4-8, Paul wants the church to understand that when we are "grieved," or wronged, by someone, instead of retaliating, God wants us to forgive and restore this person so that the enemy cannot swallow them up.

Many people use the liberty that we feel in the Spirit to abuse one another. In Galatians 5:13-14 we see that if we abuse the liberty that God gave us, we become spiritual cannibals. I have been to many churches where on the surface they appeared (in dress) to be in agreement with holiness, but there was an undertow of envy, jealousy, and bitterness. People were talking about and against each other. They were biting and devouring one another. Paul said if you allow this to continue in your church, eventually everyone will be consumed. We must guard our churches and especially our new converts, so that they enter a place of love, not destruction.

Unity comes through love. Ephesians 4:2-3 (NIV) states: *" Be completely humble and gentle; be patient, bearing with one another in love. Make every effort to keep the unity of the Spirit through the bond of peace."* There are four things mentioned that we must be consistently working on in our relationship with others. When we do these four things, then we are making the right effort to produce unity. Let's define these and see how we can implement them into relationships that we have.

To be *humble* is to have no thought of ourselves. To be without pride and instead think of others. A humble person doesn't have to have the spotlight. They are always consumed with how they can lift up others. This type of spirit, when dealing with one another, will always produce more love and unity. When others feel valued they will then turn and share that to others.

A *gentle* spirit means they are unwilling to provoke others. This person will hold their tongue instead of speaking evil against someone. They will offer kindness in the face of hatred. They will not stir up strife and contention. A gentle spirit is also known as a meek spirit and is unwilling to provoke others. It looks for opportunities to help others, to strengthen and bless others. When produce a gentle spirit as you deal with people, you are increasing the love and unity around you.

To be *patient* is to be able to bear offenses. It means not being easily provoked by others. A person who is patient can bear things without thoughts of revenge. Jesus used the word *longsuffering* throughout the Bible to indicate a person who was patient. When a patient person is mistreated, their instinct is to wait and bear the offense. Their hope is that the relationship can be made right over time. We live in a world that is quickly and easily offended. This is a sign of the last days that we see described in Matthew 24. In verse 10, Jesus tells us the spirit that we see prevalent today. *"And then shall many be offended, and shall betray one another, and shall hate one another."* What God desires from His people is the opposite of what we see in the world today. When we allow a patient spirit to overtake us, then we will not be easily provoked by others. And when hard times do come, we will be able to bear those times without thought of revenge. If you need an example of this, all you need to do is study the actions of Jesus through His trial and crucifixion. He was patient through the pain. He was forgiving through the anger. He showed us the true meaning of the word *patient*. He did all of that because He loved us. When you feel the need to strike back at others, just recall His love for you and the patience that He exhibited and example Him.

And the fourth thing is to *bear with love*. This means you remember that you love the person and that is why you keep a humble, gentle and patient spirit in the face of offense. If you have to bear an offense without having a spirit of love attached to it, you will eventually fail. But we often bear many hurts from family, friends and fellow Christians, simply because we remember that we have a deeper relationship with them. It is based on the love that we have for one another. You can bear a lot when you keep love at the center of your relationship.

We see that if we are working to produce these four things in our lives when it comes to dealing with others, then love is produced and through love we are working to keep unity as well. Unity is our greatest example of love in action.

In fact in Colossians 2:2 we see a very unique phrase used to describe how we should love one another. He says we should be *knit together in love*. Even though yarn is soft and doesn't seem to have much power as a single strand, when it is knitted together something happens. It becomes something exceedingly strong and difficult to tear apart. To destroy a knitted garment you must either unravel it from the beginning or cut it. You cannot break a knitted garment. If we can knit ourselves together with love, then it will be very hard to tear us apart. And the beauty of a knitted garment is that the more you knit, the stronger it grows. The more we love and include people in our church, the harder it is to break our unity. We need to work to keep love activated through humility, gentleness and patience. And then see our love in action through the unity that will be produced.

Inward Holiness

Carla Burton

Chapter 5

The Next Step

Outward Holiness

Inward Holiness is the second step in the process of holiness. We must make sure that we are working very hard to produce inward holiness in our lives. It is going to take abstaining from some things but then we see the fruit that is produced in love and unity. Then after we achieve the right attitude and understand the underlying principles for holiness, we are to begin to apply those to our bodies through outward holiness. Jesus clearly tells the Pharisees to clean up their inward parts or their outward holiness is in vain. Remember that inward holiness produces outward fruit. I must be striving each day of my life to keep a right spirit, to renew my mind from carnality to spirituality, to actively produce the fruit of the spirit, not just shunning the works of the flesh, and to guard my tongue and my witness. God desires truth in our inward parts, and it is our responsibility to maintain not only our outward man but our inward man as well.

Heavenly Reward

In Hebrews 12:14, Paul says, "Follow peace with all men, and holiness**, *without which no man shall see the Lord.*" In the process of "following" Christ, our reward at the end of this life is to see the Lord and be in His presence. Many people allow the standards of holiness to block their view of the reward of holiness. Remember that we don't live for this present world, but for the world to come. Holiness is our ticket into the presence of God.

Made in the USA
Middletown, DE
28 March 2019